# Spelling & Phonics Age 6-7

D1586804

**Shareen Mayers**

In a strange place, not too far from here, lives a scare of monsters.

A 'scare' is what some people call a group of monsters, but these monsters are really very friendly once you get to know them.

They are a curious bunch – they look very unusual, but they are quite like you and me, and they love learning new things and having fun.

In this book you will go on a learning journey with the monsters and you are sure to have lots of fun along the way.

Do not forget to visit our website to find out more about all the monsters and to send us photos of you in your monster mask or the monsters that you draw and make!

# Contents

# oa and ou

Otto is helping Grandpa fix Poggo's skate**boa**rd.
Poggo wants to play **ou**tside.
They had better fix it quickly before it becomes cl**ou**dy!

The sounds **oa** and **ou** usually appear in the middle of words.
A t**oa**d cro**a**ks.
A m**ou**se makes a squeaking s**ou**nd.

**1** Draw a line between the rhyming pairs of words.
Write the words that rhyme.
The first one has been done for you.

| | |
|---|---|
| boat | soak |
| road | coat |
| toast | groan |
| moan | coast |
| cloak | toad |

<u>boat</u>    <u>coat</u>

_____  _____

_____  _____

_____  _____

**2** Say each sound and then blend the sounds together to read the words.
Write the whole words you make.

**a** a→b→ou→t = _____

**c** s→ou→n→d = _____

**b** c→l→ou→d = _____

**d** a→m→ou→n→t = _____

**3** Complete each word with either **oa** or **ou**.
Write the word you make underneath.
The first one has been done for you.

a 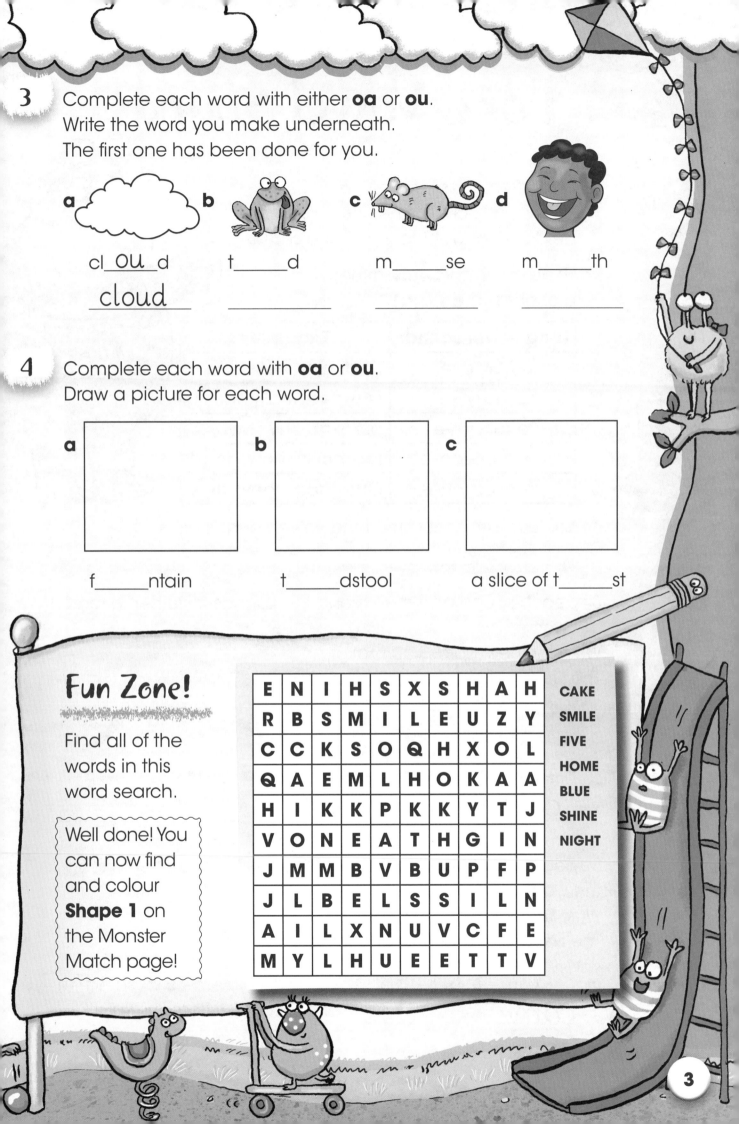 b    c    d

cl_ou_d    t____d    m____se    m____th

cloud    _____    _____    _____

**4** Complete each word with **oa** or **ou**.
Draw a picture for each word.

a    b    c

f____ntain    t____dstool    a slice of t____st

# Long Vowel Sounds

Dad often goes into the c**a**v**e**.
He uses a torch that has b**ee**n fixed by Otto.
He does not want to trip over a sn**a**k**e**.

There are **five vowels** in the
alphabet (**a e i o u**).

| Long vowel sounds | Examples |
|---|---|
| ai, ay, a–e | sn**ai**l, d**ay**, c**a**k**e** |
| ee, ea, y, e–e | s**ee**, p**ea**, reall**y**, th**e**s**e** |
| ie, igh, y, i–e | p**ie**, s**igh**, sh**y**, f**i**v**e** |
| oe, oa, ow, o–e | t**oe**, b**oa**t, sn**ow**, h**o**m**e** |
| ue, oo, ew, u–e | cl**ue**, f**oo**d, ch**ew**, t**u**n**e** |

You can see that some long vowel sounds are split.

**1** Say each sound and then blend the sounds together to read
the words.
Write the new words you make.
The first one has been done for you.

a    b    c    d

c→a→k→e     l→a→k→e     r→a→k→e     sh→a→k→e

cake _____ _____ _____

**2** Say each sound and then blend the sounds together to read
the words.
Write the new words you make.
The first one has been done for you.

a c→a→m→e   b s→a→m→e   c b→l→a→m→e d sh→a→m→e

came _____ _____ _____

**3** Draw a line between the rhyming pairs of words.
Write the words that rhyme.
The first one has been done for you.

| | |
|---|---|
| side | hive |
| rise | smile |
| pile | wide |
| five | wise |

_side_   _wide_

_____   _____

_____   _____

_____   _____

**4** Choose words from the box that rhyme with the given words.
Write down the rhyming words.

| like | fine | side | hike | file | wide |
|------|------|------|------|------|------|
| shine | hide | mile | nine | bike | smile |

**a** Words that rhyme with glide _____

**b** Words that rhyme with pile _____

**c** Words that rhyme with pike _____

**d** Words that rhyme with pine _____

# Fun Zone!

Make a money box to keep your pocket money in.

Congratulations! You can now find and colour **Shape 2** on the Monster Match page!

**Monster Money Box**

You will need a shoebox, scissors, paint, white paper, crayons, glitter and glue.

Ask an adult to help when needed.

1 Paint the outside of the box and lid. Leave to dry.
2 On the white paper draw a monster face and decorate with glitter. Cut a hole in the monster face for the mouth.
3 Glue the monster face onto the top of the lid. Cut the mouth out of the lid.
4 Place the lid on the box.

# -y

Kora loves going to a party.
Tizz and Fizz love part**ies** too.

The letter **y** can be found at the end of words.

fl**y**     The **y** in some words sounds like **ie** (as in pie).

bab**y**     The **y** in some words sounds like **ee** (as in tree).

To make a **y** word plural, **y** is changed to an **i** before adding **-es**.

| Singular | Plural |
|---|---|
| fl**y** | fl**ies** |

| Singular | Plural |
|---|---|
| bab**y** | bab**ies** |

**1** Add **y** to complete each word.
Write the new word.
The first one has been done for you.

**a** bab**y** <u>baby</u>      **e** b__  _____      **i** lad__  _____

**b** m__  _____      **f** bod__  _____      **j** cr__  _____

**c** tin__  _____      **g** tr__  _____      **k** cop__  _____

**d** fl__  _____      **h** hand__  _____      **l** wh__  _____

**2** Add **-es** to these words.
Remember to change the **y** to an **i** before adding **-es**.
The first one has been done for you.

**a** baby <u>babies</u>      **c** reply _____      **e** lady _____

**b** fly _____      **d** party _____      **f** army _____

**3** Lots of weather words end in **y**.
Write the correct word under each picture.

| foggy | sunny | rainy | snowy |

**a** 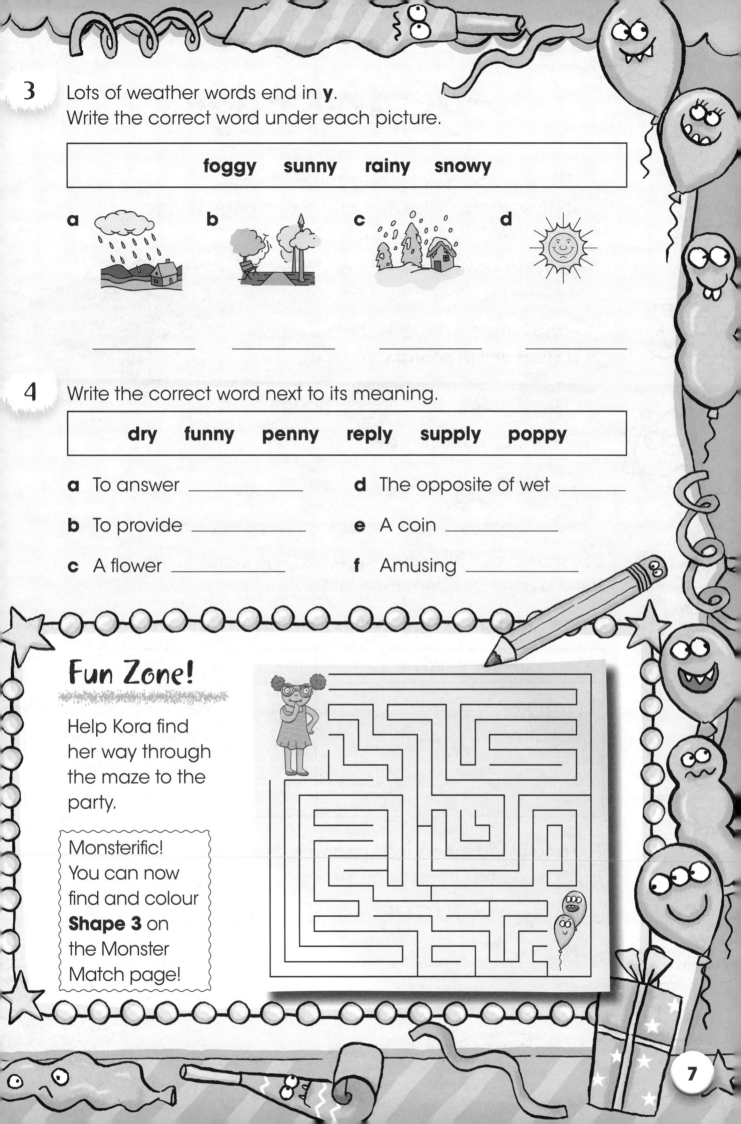  **b**  **c**  **d**

_____  _____  _____  _____

**4** Write the correct word next to its meaning.

| dry | funny | penny | reply | supply | poppy |

**a** To answer _____

**d** The opposite of wet _____

**b** To provide _____

**e** A coin _____

**c** A flower _____

**f** Amusing _____

## Fun Zone!

Help Kora find her way through the maze to the party.

Monsterific! You can now find and colour **Shape 3** on the Monster Match page!

# -ge and -dge

Otto is in char**ge** of taking Zak for a walk.
They walk along the river and over a hu**ge** bri**dge**.
They have to be careful near the e**dge**.

**-ge** and **-dge** at the end of words
make a **j** (as in jam) sound.

**-dge** is used if the letter before makes
a **short vowel sound** (a e i o u).

fu**dge**          ba**dge**

Other words end in **-ge**.

chan**ge**          ca**ge**

**1** Sort the words below into **-dge** and **-ge** words in the table.
The first one has been done for you.

**fudge   charge   edge   wage   bridge   huge   village   dodge**

| -dge words | -ge words |
|---|---|
| fudge | |

**2** Say and blend the sounds and write the words.
The first one has been done for you.

**a** fu+dge   = <u>fudge</u>          **d** ba+dge   = _____

**b** bri+dge  = _____          **e** e+dge    = _____

**c** do+dge   = _____          **f** he+dge   = _____

**3** Say and blend the sounds and write the words.
The first one has been done for you.

**a** hu+ge = _huge_

**b** a+ge = _____

**c** ra+ge = _____

**d** chan+ge = _____

**e** bul+ge = _____

**f** stran+ge = _____

**4** Choose the correct **–ge** or **–dge** endings for these words.
Write the words you make below.
The first one has been done for you.

**a** hu _ge_
_huge_

**c** bri _____
_____

**b** ra _____
_____

**d** he _____
_____

## Fun Zone!

Make your own monster badge.

That looks great! You can now find and colour **Shape 4** on the Monster Match page!

### Monster Badge

You will need card, crayons, scissors, a safety pin and tape.

Ask an adult to help when needed.

1 Draw the outline of a monster face on a piece of card.
2 Cut this out.
3 Colour the monster face.
4 Turn it over and tape a safety pin to the back.

# -ed and -ing Endings

Last week, Otto fix**ed** Litmus's calculator.
Yesterday it broke again.
Now he is busy fix**ing** it for Litmus to use.

**Suffixes** are groups of letters that can be **added to the ends of words**.

|  | Root word | Past tense (-ed) | Present tense (-ing) |
|---|---|---|---|
| Simply add the suffix **-ed** or **-ing** to the end of a word. | look | look**ed** | look**ing** |
| If a word ends in **e**, **drop the e** and add **-ed** or **-ing**. | smile | smil**ed** | smil**ing** |
| If a word contains a **short vowel sound** and one ending letter, **double the final letters** first. | stop | sto**pp**ed | sto**pp**ing |

You do not double the letter x → fix, fixed and fixing!

**1** Add **-ing** to these root words and then put them in the box. Some examples have been done for you.

enjoy    hug    jump    share    mix    clap    like    bake    chat

| Add -ing | Drop the e and add -ing | Double the last letter and add -ing |
|---|---|---|
| enjoying | sharing | clapping |

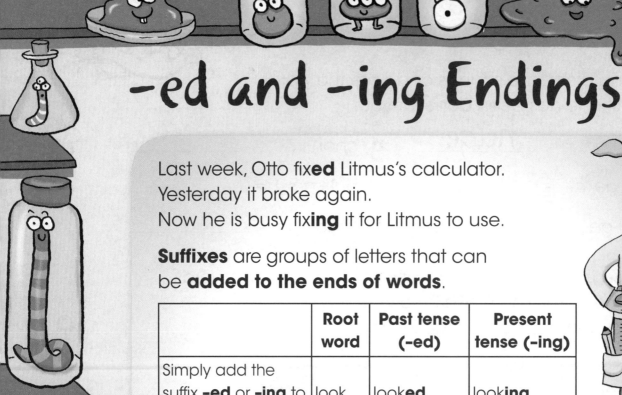

**2** Add **-ed** to these words.
Write the new words you make.
The first one has been done for you.

**a**

hug _ged_
_hugged_

**c**

clap _____

_____

**b**

lift _____

_____

**d**

pull _____

_____

**3** Fill in the sentences below using the correct words from the box.

| riding    smiled    shouting    baked |
| --- |

**a** I like _____ on my bike.

**b** Tizz was _____ across the playground.

**c** Fizz _____ at Tizz because she was happy.

**d** Dad _____ a delicious cake.

## Fun Zone!

Circle the two identical pictures of Leckie.

Well done! You can now find and colour **Shape 5** on the Monster Match page!

# -er and -est Endings

Poggo loves skateboarding.
He is fast**er** at skateboarding than Litmus.
Poggo is the fast**est** monster at skateboarding.

| | Root word | Add –er | Add –est |
|---|---|---|---|
| Add the suffix **–er** to compare two things and **–est** to compare more than two things. | fast | fast**er** | fast**est** |
| If the adjective contains a **short vowel sound**, **double the final letter** and add the suffix. | hot | hott**er** | hott**est** |
| If the adjective ends in a **y**, change the **y** to an **i** and add the suffix. | happy | happ**ier** | happ**iest** |

**1** Add **–est** to the words below.
The first one has been done for you.

| | Root word | –er | –est |
|---|---|---|---|
| **a** | tall | taller | tallest |
| **b** | cold | colder | _____ |
| **c** | short | shorter | _____ |
| **d** | big | bigger | _____ |
| **e** | thin | thinner | _____ |
| **f** | funny | funnier | _____ |
| **g** | lucky | luckier | _____ |

**2** Change these words back to their root words.
The first one has been done for you.

**a** taller/tallest    tall    **e** thinner/thinnest _____

**b** colder/coldest _____    **f** funnier/funniest _____

**c** shorter/shortest _____    **g** luckier/luckiest _____

**d** bigger/biggest _____    **h** drier/driest _____

**3** Sort the words below into the correct boxes.
One has been done for you.

**taller thinner shorter bigger funnier luckier colder drier**

| Add –er | Double the final letter and add –er | Change the y to an i and add –er |
|---|---|---|
| | | drier |

## Fun Zone!

Turn some normal letters into monster letters!

Congratulations! You can now find and colour **Shape 6** on the Monster Match page!

### Monster Letters

You will need white paper, coloured paper, crayons and glue.

Ask an adult to help when needed.

1 Draw a letter on the white paper. This could be 'm' for monster!
2 Use crayons to decorate your monster letter with patterns, shapes, teeth and eyes. Allow to dry.
3 Cut the letter out and stick it on a coloured piece of paper.
4 You can make more monster letters. Can you make all the letters in your name?

# Monster Challenge 1

**1** Circle the **i-e** sound in these words.
The first one has been done for you.

**a** l(i)k(e)

**g** fine

**b** hike

**h** side

**c** file

**i** shine

**d** wide

**j** smile

**e** nine

**k** bike

**f** mile

**l** hide

**2** Underline the words with the **o-e** sound.
Remember to say the words first so you can hear the sound.
One has been done for you.

home

ride

woke

hole

came

mope

time

tune

hope

**3** Choose either **-dge** or **-ge** to complete each word.
The first one has been done for you.

**a** The man walked across the bri_dge_.

**b** The boy sat near the e_____ of the water.

**c** Tizz has a hu_____ house.

**d** Fizz saw a stran_____ cat near the house.

**4** Sort these words into two sets.
The first one has been done for you.

baby    cry    why    lady    reply    copy

lorry    supply    tiny    multiply    rely    sunny

| Words in which the y sounds like ee | Words in which the y sounds like ie |
|---|---|
| baby | |

**5** Change these words back to their root word.
The first one has been done for you.

**a** cries → _____cry_____    **d** copies → _____

**b** ladies → _____    **e** supplies → _____

**c** replies → _____    **f** multiplies → _____

**6** Complete the table below.
Remember to change the **y** to an **i** and add **-er** or **-est**.

| Root word | Add -er | Add -est |
|---|---|---|
| funny | funnier | |
| happy | | happiest |
| lucky | luckier | |
| cheeky | | cheekiest |

# -le

Mum has asked Otto to look after litt**le** Nano.
She has left some food on the tab**le**.
There is a bott**le** of milk for Nano and an
app**le** for Otto.

Some words end in **-le**.
Some words have **short vowel sounds**
and **double letters** before **-le**.

```
            ┌──────── Double letters ────────┐
            ↓           ↓             ↓
        bo**tt**le     li**tt**le    pu**dd**le
            ↑           ↑             ↑
            └─── Short vowel sound (u as in put) ───┘
```

Other words have **long vowel sounds** and **one letter**
before **-le**.

```
            ┌──────── One letter ────────┐
            ↓           ↓             ↓
        ta**b**le     nee**d**le    peo**p**le ('eo' is the tricky bit in this
                                     word but it still makes the 'ee' sound!)
```

**1** Put the words below into the correct boxes.
The first one has been done for you.

| apple | noodle | giggle | sparkle |
|-------|--------|--------|---------|
| sizzle | beetle | battle | needle |

| Double letter before -le | One letter before -le |
|--------------------------|------------------------|
| apple | |

**2**    Write the words next to the picture.
Use the words in **1** to help you.

a   _____

c   _____

b   _____

d   _____

**3**    Underline the **-le** words in the poem below.
Write the **-le** words below.
The first one has been done for you.

The cat fell into a <u>puddle</u>,

And got into a muddle,

Then he began to giggle,

Which makes him wriggle and wiggle!

puddle _____ _____

_____ _____

## Fun Zone!

Follow the alphabet
to make the picture.

Congratulations!
You can now find
and colour **Shape
7** on the Monster
Match page!

# s Sounds

Fizz and Litmus are having
a bi**cy**cle race.
Whoever finishes first is
the best **cy**clist.
Litmus fell off his bi**cy**cle!
His shoela**ce**s came undone!

In some words the **s sound**
can be spelt with a **c**.

| **s sound** spelt as<br>**c** before **e** (**ce**) | **s sound** spelt as<br>**c** before **i** (**ci**) | **s sound** spelt as<br>**c** before **y** (**cy**) |
| --- | --- | --- |
| rac**e** | **ci**rcle | bi**cy**cle |

---

**1** These words have been mixed up.
Write the words in the correct boxes.
The first one has been done for you.

cell   cereal   centre   circle   ice   decide   city   price

| ce words | ci words |
| --- | --- |
| cell | |

**2**  Underline the **cy** in the words below.

    **a** fancy        **b** mercy        **c** bicycle        **d** cyclist

**3**  Choose the correctly spelt word for each sentence.
Write it in the space in each sentence.

    **a**  Kora wore a (fancy/fansi) _____ dress to the party.

    **b**  Tizz ate some (ise/ice) _____ cream.

    **c**  Poggo rode his (bisycle/bicycle) _____ to school.

    **d**  Litmus ate some (cereal/sereal) _____ for breakfast.

    **e**  Fizz tied her (shoelaces/shoelases) _____ before playing basketball.

# Fun Zone!

It is time to make some messy monsters!

That is a marvellous monster! You can now find and colour **Shape 8** on the Monster Match page!

**Messy Monsters**

You will need green tissue paper, coloured paper, scissors and glue.

Ask an adult to help when needed.

1 Cut the paper into a monster body, head, two arms and two legs.
2 Glue the body, head, arms and legs onto coloured paper.
3 Cut up the tissue paper into long, thin strips. Shape the strips into small balls.
4 Add glue to the monster body and add the balls of tissue paper.
5 Cut out some eyes and a mouth from the coloured paper and glue them onto the tissue paper. Leave to dry.

# -ful and -ness Endings

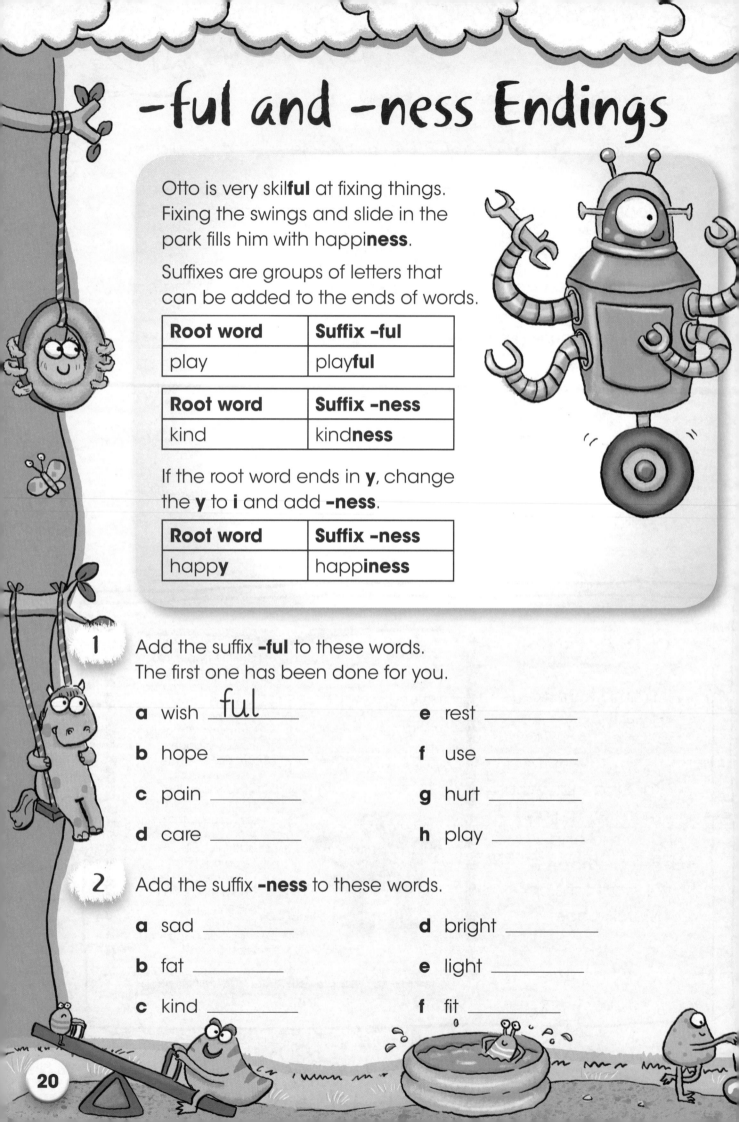

Otto is very skil**ful** at fixing things. Fixing the swings and slide in the park fills him with happi**ness**.

Suffixes are groups of letters that can be added to the ends of words.

| Root word | Suffix -ful |
|-----------|-------------|
| play      | play**ful** |

| Root word | Suffix -ness |
|-----------|--------------|
| kind      | kind**ness** |

If the root word ends in **y**, change the **y** to **i** and add **-ness**.

| Root word | Suffix -ness  |
|-----------|---------------|
| happ**y** | happ**iness**  |

**1** Add the suffix **-ful** to these words.
The first one has been done for you.

**a** wish __ful__

**b** hope _____

**c** pain _____

**d** care _____

**e** rest _____

**f** use _____

**g** hurt _____

**h** play _____

**2** Add the suffix **-ness** to these words.

**a** sad _____

**b** fat _____

**c** kind _____

**d** bright _____

**e** light _____

**f** fit _____

**3** Change the **y** to an **i** and add **–ness** to these words.
The first one has been done for you.

a happy ___happiness___     e silly _____

b funny _____     f tricky _____

c empty _____     g nasty _____

d lazy _____      h crazy _____

**4** Add **–ful** or **–ness** to complete these sentences.

a Zak was very play_____ with the frisbee.

b The book had use_____ pictures of wildlife.

c The children had a rest_____ break over the summer.

d The ladies visited the fit_____ club.

## Fun Zone!

Find five differences between these two pictures of Gran.

That is great! You can now find and colour **Shape 9** on the Monster Match page!

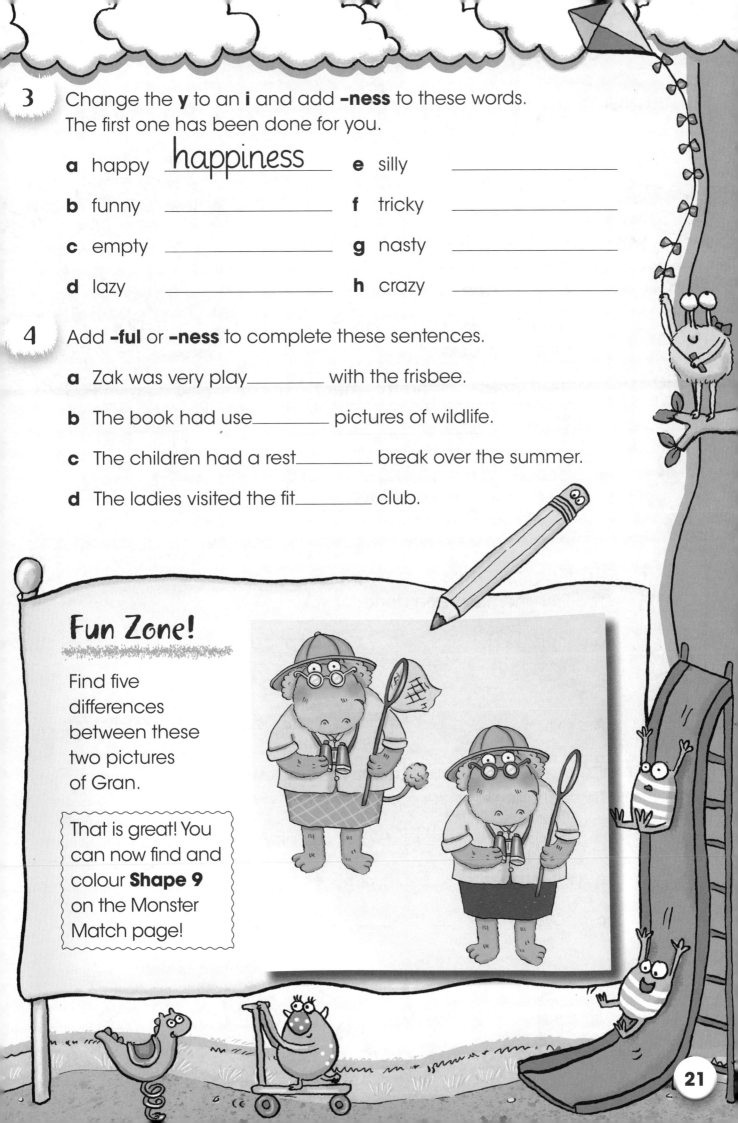

# -ment and -less Endings

Gran is in the wild wood collecting some mini-monsters.
She hears a move**ment** in the trees.
She is not scared though.
She is fear**less**!

**-ment** or **-less** can be added to the end of words.

| Root word | Suffix -ment |
|-----------|--------------|
| enjoy     | enjoy**ment** |

| Root word | Suffix -less |
|-----------|--------------|
| care      | care**less**  |

**1** Add the suffix **-less** to these words.
The first one has been done for you.

**a** hope _less_          **d** price _____

**b** fear _____        **e** end _____

**c** shame _____       **f** speech _____

**2** Change these words back to their root words.
The first one has been done for you.

**a** enjoyment → _enjoy_     **d** payment → _____

**b** agreement → _____   **e** excitement → _____

**c** movement → _____    **f** treatment → _____

**3** Write the correct word under each picture.

| pavement | agreement | movement | payment |
|----------|-----------|----------|---------|

a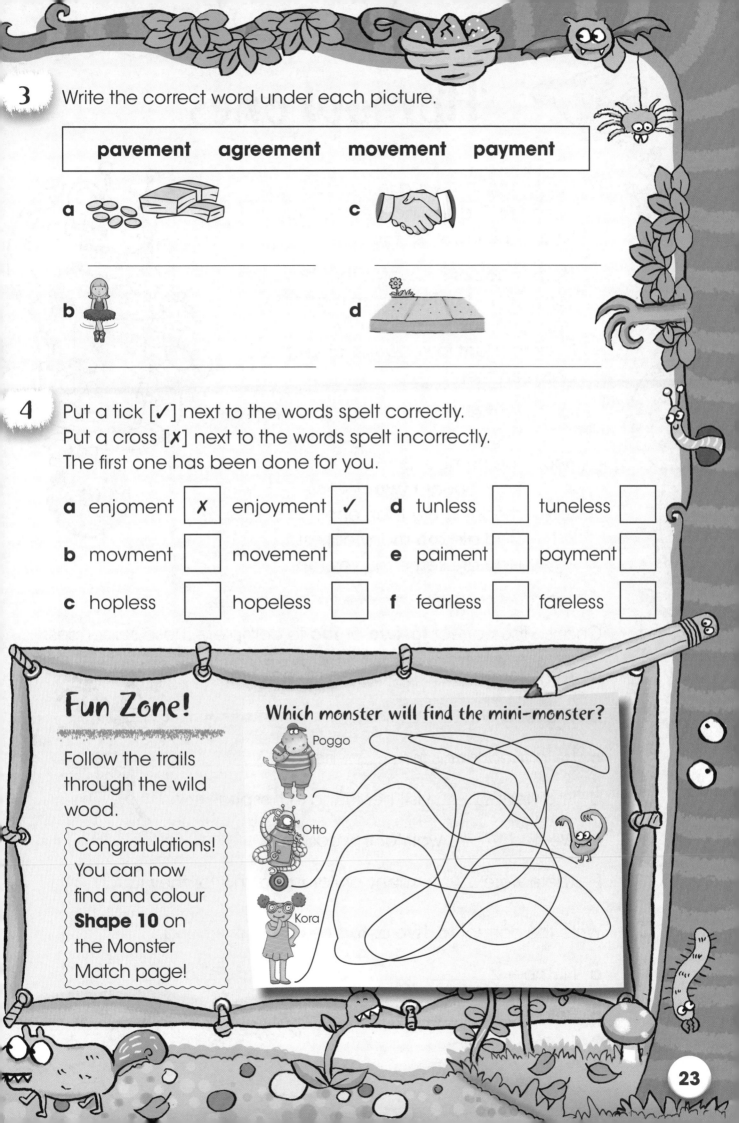

_____

c

_____

b

_____

d

_____

**4** Put a tick [✓] next to the words spelt correctly.
Put a cross [✗] next to the words spelt incorrectly.
The first one has been done for you.

a enjoment [✗]  enjoyment [✓]    d tunless [ ]  tuneless [ ]

b movment [ ]  movement [ ]    e paiment [ ]  payment [ ]

c hopless [ ]  hopeless [ ]    f fearless [ ]  fareless [ ]

# Fun Zone!

Follow the trails
through the wild
wood.

Congratulations!
You can now
find and colour
**Shape 10** on
the Monster
Match page!

**Which monster will find the mini-monster?**

Poggo

Otto

Kora

# Homophones

I am fixing the swing in the park.
I need **to** find **two** nails in the toolbox.
I need the hammer **too**!

**Homophones** are words that have the same sound but **different** meanings and spellings.
It is important to know the difference between them!

**to** – comes before a verb (a doing word)
Poggo wanted **to go** home.
**two** – the number 2
Kora bought **two** books.
**too** – means more than enough or also
Dad ate **too** many cakes!
Dad ate some apples **too**!

**1** Choose the correct **to**, **two** or **too** to complete these sentences.

**a** They bought _____ bicycles at the shop.

**b** The food was _____ salty.

**c** He played tennis for _____ hours.

**d** She went _____ visit her friend in hospital.

**e** We had _____ wait for the coach.

**f** There were _____ many children waiting for their lunch.

**2** Write the correct **to**, **two** or **too** next to its meaning.

**a** Number 2 _____      **c** More than/also _____

**b** Before a verb _____

**3** Write the correct homophone for the picture.
The first one has been done for you.

**a** see/sea

sea

**d** night/knight

_____

**b** sun/son

_____

**e** be/bee

_____

**c** one/won

**1**

_____

**f** write/right

_____

**4** Choose the correct homophone.
Write it in the space provided.

**a** Poggo visited the (see/sea)_____ and

(ate/eight)_____ ice cream.

**b** The buzzing (be/bee)_____ was noisy

last (night/knight)_____.

**c** The author wanted to (write/right)_____ a

(new/knew)_____ book.

**d** When Tizz came (to/too)_____ visit, she had not

(won/one)_____ but (two/too)_____ drinks!

## Fun Zone!

Start with the first letter then cross
out every other letter to find out
the name of each monster.

Well done! You can now find
and colour **Shape 11** on the
Monster Match page!

P R O C G I G E O X

_____

L Y I R T D M O U X S

_____

K A O B R Z A Q

_____

# Contractions (')

Grandpa needs Otto to go shopping for him.
Otto doesn't like shopping.
He'll have to buy everything on the shopping list.
He can't find the food for Leckie!

In **contractions**, an **apostrophe** (') is used to show where letters have been taken out and the two words are joined together (contracted).

| Full word | Contraction | Letters missing |
|---|---|---|
| can**no**t | can't | missing no |
| did n**o**t | didn't | missing o |
| has n**o**t | hasn't | missing o |
| he **wi**ll | he'll | missing wi |
| they **a**re | they're | missing a |

**1** Write out each contraction in full.
The first one has been done for you.

**a** I'm   = _I am_          **e** they're = _____

**b** I'll   = _____   **f** aren't  = _____

**c** she'll = _____   **g** we're   = _____

**d** isn't  = _____   **h** hasn't  = _____

**2** Put a tick [✓] next to the word where the apostrophe has been used correctly.
The first one has been done for you.

**a** couldn't [✓]  could'nt [ ]    **d** youv'e [ ]  you've [ ]

**b** shouldn't [ ]  should'nt [ ]    **e** I'd [ ]  'Id [ ]

**c** would'nt [ ]  wouldn't [ ]    **f** your'e [ ]  you're [ ]

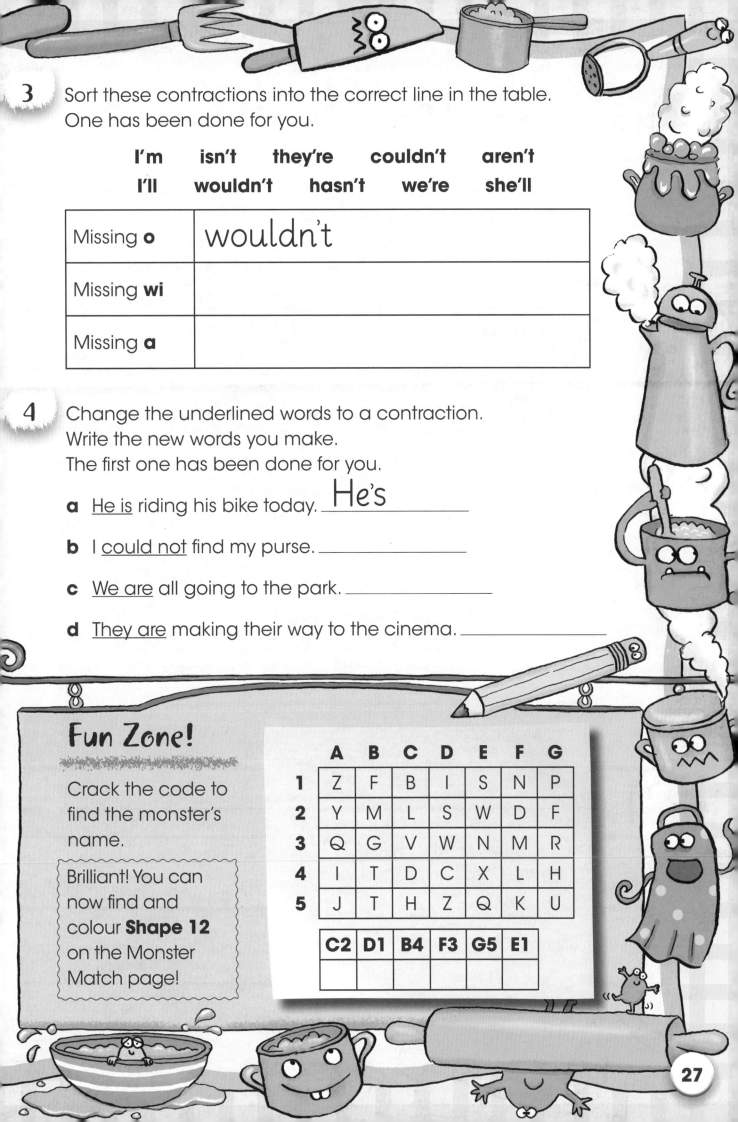

**3** Sort these contractions into the correct line in the table. One has been done for you.

| | | | | | |
|---|---|---|---|---|---|
| **I'm** | **isn't** | **they're** | **couldn't** | **aren't** | |
| **I'll** | **wouldn't** | **hasn't** | **we're** | **she'll** | |

| | |
|---|---|
| Missing **o** | wouldn't |
| Missing **wi** | |
| Missing **a** | |

**4** Change the underlined words to a contraction. Write the new words you make. The first one has been done for you.

**a** <u>He is</u> riding his bike today. ___He's___

**b** I <u>could not</u> find my purse. _____

**c** <u>We are</u> all going to the park. _____

**d** <u>They are</u> making their way to the cinema. _____

## Fun Zone!

Crack the code to find the monster's name.

Brilliant! You can now find and colour **Shape 12** on the Monster Match page!

| | A | B | C | D | E | F | G |
|---|---|---|---|---|---|---|---|
| **1** | Z | F | B | I | S | N | P |
| **2** | Y | M | L | S | W | D | F |
| **3** | Q | G | V | W | N | M | R |
| **4** | I | T | D | C | X | L | H |
| **5** | J | T | H | Z | Q | K | U |

| C2 | D1 | B4 | F3 | G5 | E1 |
|---|---|---|---|---|---|
| | | | | | |

27

# Monster Challenge 2

**1** Choose the correct word from the box and write it under the picture.
The first one has been done for you.

| ice   bicycle   circle   bouncy   mice   cereal |

**a**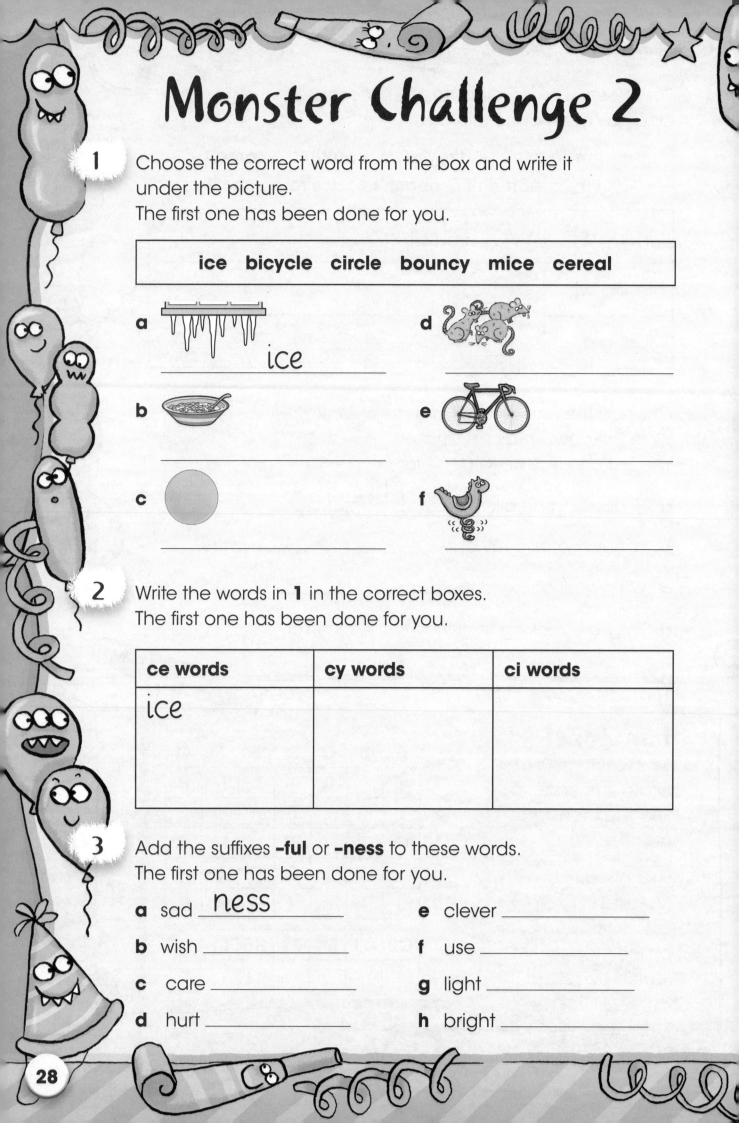
_ice_

**b**

**c**

**d**

**e**

**f**

**2** Write the words in **1** in the correct boxes.
The first one has been done for you.

| ce words | cy words | ci words |
|----------|----------|----------|
| ice      |          |          |

**3** Add the suffixes **–ful** or **–ness** to these words.
The first one has been done for you.

**a** sad _ness_

**b** wish _____

**c** care _____

**d** hurt _____

**e** clever _____

**f** use _____

**g** light _____

**h** bright _____

**4** Add the suffixes **–ment** or **–less** to these words.
The first one has been done for you.

**a** enjoy _ment_

**e** end _____

**b** pave _____

**f** pay _____

**c** care _____

**g** move _____

**d** price _____

**h** rest _____

**5** Sort the words in **4** into the correct boxes.
The first one has been done for you.

| –less words | –ment words |
|---|---|
|  | enjoyment |

**6** Add the apostrophe to make these contractions.
The first one has been done for you.

**a** Im = _I'm_

**g** hasnt = _____

**b** Ill = _____

**h** couldnt = _____

**c** shell = _____

**i** shouldnt = _____

**d** isnt = _____

**j** youve = _____

**e** theyre = _____

**k** Id = _____

**f** arent = _____

**l** youre = _____

I knew you could do it!

You have made it to the end of the book.

You are a magnificent monster!

# Answers

**Page 2**
1 boat–coat; road–toad; toast–coast; moan–groan; cloak–soak
2 **a** about **b** cloud **c** sound **d** amount

**Page 3**
3 **a** cloud **b** toad **c** mouse **d** mouth
4 **a** fountain **b** toadstool **c** toast

## Fun zone

| | | | | | | | | |
|---|---|---|---|---|---|---|---|---|
| E | N | I | H | S | X | S | H | A | H |
| R | B | S | M | I | L | E | U | Z | Y |
| C | C | K | S | O | Q | H | X | O | L |
| Q | A | E | M | L | H | O | K | A | A |
| H | I | K | K | P | K | K | Y | T | J |
| V | O | N | E | A | T | H | G | I | N |
| J | M | M | B | V | B | U | P | F | P |
| J | L | B | E | L | S | S | I | L | N |
| A | I | L | X | N | U | V | C | F | E |
| M | Y | L | H | U | E | E | T | T | V |

**Page 4**
1 **a** cake **b** lake **c** rake **d** shake
2 **a** came **b** same **c** blame **d** shame

**Page 5**
3 side–wide, rise–wise, pile–smile, five–hive
4 **a** wide, side, hide  **c** like, hike, bike
  **b** file, mile, smile  **d** nine, fine, shine

**Page 6**
1 **a** baby **c** tiny **e** by  **g** try  **i** lady **k** copy
  **b** my  **d** fly **f** body **h** handy **j** cry **l** why
2 **a** babies  **c** replies  **e** ladies
  **b** flies  **d** parties  **f** armies

**Page 7**
3 **a** rainy **b** foggy **c** snowy **d** sunny
4 **a** reply  **c** poppy **e** penny
  **b** supply **d** dry  **f** funny

## Fun zone

**Page 8**
1

| -dge words | -ge words |
|---|---|
| fudge | charge |
| edge | wage |
| bridge | huge |
| dodge | village |

2 **a** fudge  **c** dodge  **e** edge
  **b** bridge  **d** badge  **f** hedge

**Page 9**
3 **a** huge  **c** rage  **e** bulge
  **b** age  **d** change **f** strange
4 **a** huge **b** rage **c** bridge **d** hedge

**Page 10**
1

| Add –ing | Drop the e and add –ing | Double the last letter and add –ing |
|---|---|---|
| enjoying | sharing | clapping |
| jumping | liking | chatting |
| mixing | baking | hugging |

**Page 11**
2 **a** hugged **b** lifted **c** clapped **d** pulled
3 **a** riding **b** shouting (or riding) **c** smiled
  **d** baked

## Fun zone

**Page 12**
1 **a** tallest  **c** shortest **e** thinnest **g** luckiest
  **b** coldest **d** biggest **f** funniest

**Page 13**
2 **a** tall  **c** short  **e** thin  **g** luck
  **b** cold  **d** big  **f** fun  **h** dry
3

| Add –er | Double the final letter and add –er | Change the y to an i and add –er |
|---|---|---|
| taller | thinner | drier |
| shorter | bigger | funnier |
| colder | | luckier |

**Page 14**
1 **a** like  **g** fine
  **b** hike  **h** side
  **c** file  **i** shine
  **d** wide  **j** smile
  **e** nine  **k** bike
  **f** mile  **l** hide
2 **Underlined words:** home, hope, mope, hole, woke
3 **a** bridge **b** edge **c** huge **d** strange

**Page 15**
4

| Words in which the y sounds like ee | Words in which the y sounds like ie |
|---|---|
| baby lady copy lorry tiny sunny | cry why reply supply multiply rely |

5 **a** cry **b** lady **c** reply **d** copy **e** supply
  **f** multiply
6 **Add -er:** happier, cheekier
  **Add -est:** funniest, luckiest

30

## Page 16

**1**

| Double letter before –le | One letter before –le |
| --- | --- |
| apple | noodle |
| giggle | sparkle |
| sizzle | beetle |
| battle | needle |

## Page 17

**2** **a** beetle **b** needle **c** apple **d** giggle

**3** **Correctly underlined** – puddle, muddle, giggle, wriggle, wiggle

### Fun zone

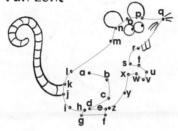

## Page 18

**1**

| ce words | | ci words |
| --- | --- | --- |
| cell | ice | city |
| cereal | | circle |
| centre | | decide |
| price | | |

## Page 19

**2** **a** fan<u>c</u>y **b** mer<u>c</u>y **c** bi<u>c</u>ycle **d** <u>c</u>yclist

**3** **a** fancy **c** bicycle **e** shoelaces
   **b** ice **d** cereal

## Page 20

**1** **a** wishful **d** careful **g** hurtful
   **b** hopeful **e** restful **h** playful
   **c** painful **f** useful

**2** **a** sadness **c** kindness **e** lightness
   **b** fatness **d** brightness **f** fitness

## Page 21

**3** **a** happiness **d** laziness **g** nastiness
   **b** funniness **e** silliness **h** craziness
   **c** emptiness **f** trickiness

**4** **a** ful **b** ful **c** ful **d** ness

### Fun zone

## Page 22

**1** **a** hopeless **c** shameless **e** endless
   **b** fearless **d** priceless **f** speechless

**2** **a** enjoy **c** move **e** excite
   **b** agree **d** pay **f** treat

## Page 23

**3** **a** payment **b** movement
   **c** agreement **d** pavement

**4** **a** enjoment ✗ enjoyment ✓
   **b** movment ✗ movement ✓
   **c** hopless ✗ hopeless ✓
   **d** tunless ✗ tuneless ✓
   **e** paiment ✗ payment ✓
   **f** fearless ✓ fareless ✗

### Fun zone

Otto will find the mini monster.

## Page 24

**1** **a** two **b** too **c** two **d** to **e** to **f** too

**2** **a** two **b** to **c** too

## Page 25

**3** **a** sea **c** one **e** bee
   **b** sun **d** night **f** write

**4** **a** sea; ate **c** write; new
   **b** bee; night **d** to; one; two

### Fun zone

POGGO, LITMUS, KORA

## Page 26

**1** **a** I am **c** she will **e** they are **g** we are
   **b** I will **d** is not **f** are not **h** has not

**2** **a** couldn't ✓ **c** wouldn't ✓ **e** I'd ✓
   **b** shouldn't ✓ **d** you've ✓ **f** you're ✓

## Page 27

**3** **missing o:** wouldn't, couldn't, isn't, aren't, hasn't
   **missing wi:** I'll, she'll
   **missing a:** I'm, they're, we're

**4** **a** He's **b** couldn't **c** We're **d** They're

### Fun zone

LITMUS

## Page 28

**1** **a** ice **c** circle **e** bicycle
   **b** cereal **d** mice **f** bouncy

**2**

| ce words | cy words | ci words |
| --- | --- | --- |
| ice | bicycle | circle |
| cereal | bouncy | |
| mice | | |

**3** **a** sadness **d** hurtful **g** lightness
   **b** wishful **e** cleverness **h** brightness
   **c** careful **f** useful

## Page 29

**4** **a** enjoyment **d** priceless **g** movement
   **b** pavement **e** endless **h** restless
   **c** careless **f** payment

**5** **–less words:** careless, priceless, endless, restless **–ment words:** enjoyment, pavement, payment, movement

**6** **a** I'm **e** they're **i** shouldn't
   **b** I'll **f** aren't **j** you've
   **c** she'll **g** hasn't **k** I'd
   **d** isn't **h** couldn't **l** you're

31

# Monster Match

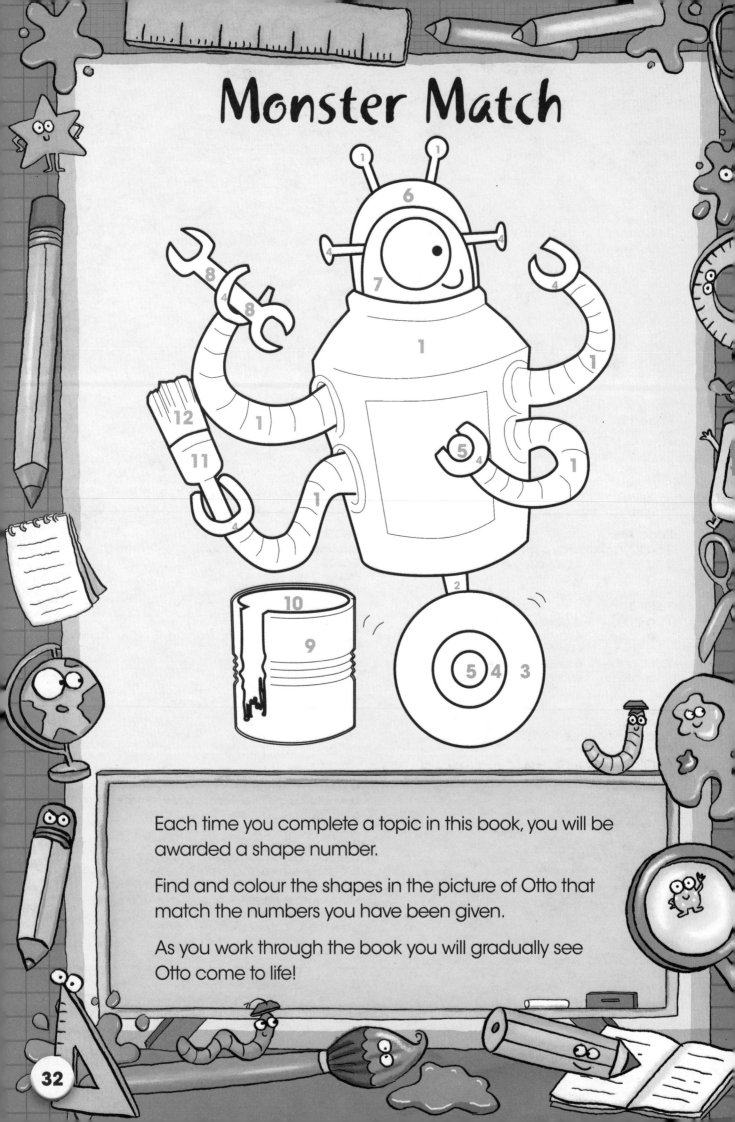

Each time you complete a topic in this book, you will be awarded a shape number.

Find and colour the shapes in the picture of Otto that match the numbers you have been given.

As you work through the book you will gradually see Otto come to life!